LOOKING FOR
Ireland

An Irish-Appalachian Pilgrimage

LAURA TREACY BENTLEY

Mountain State Press, Inc.
Charleston, WV
2017

Also by Laura Treacy Bentley

Lake Effect
A collection of poetry set in Appalachia and Ireland

The Silver Tattoo
A psychological thriller set in Ireland

Night Terrors
A short story prequel to *The Silver Tattoo*

Copyright 2017, Laura Treacy Bentley

All rights reserved.

First edition published 2017 by Mountain State Press, Inc.

Poems and photographs: Laura Treacy Bentley

Book design: Elizabeth Ford

ISBN: 978-0-941092-74-6

LCCN: 2017902313

I know this path by magic, not by sight.

PAULA MEEHAN
"The Well"

Amulets

A Scarlet Tanager beckons
the spellbound lake and garnet sun,
jeweled in a casement window.

In dark forests,
wands of mottled light
ignite slender trees.

Dactylic song sparks
from leafy canopies.
Cast on the cabin wall,

a frame of veiled heat.
My shadow moves inside
its fevered canvas.

Swans, Tundra Swans

float on a November lake
like the children of Lir
    only this flock,
        seven times over.

I hike to the furthest shore
and sketch white swans
    drifting
        on silvered currents.

Stealing toward the lake's edge,
I try to capture wild beauty
    before it
        takes flight.

The mindful swans watch
with unruffled glances
    and glide
        into deeper water.

Signs

It's that slow turn toward winter
when Chicory blossoms

fade in the ditch line,
and Black-Eyed Susans

scatter wind-borne seed.
Upturned Coltsfoot

mark a bear's silver trail,
and Queen Anne's Lace

unravels
in the wind.

Cloudbursts of leaves
dust the earth

and daffodils
remember spring.

Nights colder, the dark
comes sooner now.

Fat pumpkins for sale
at roadside stands.

Goldenrod frosts the hills.
Flocks of Starlings

begin their murmurations,
dazzling all who look up.

Late Autumn

Deep in the bear's brain
lies a vision of winter,
its beckoning silence.

Above her head,
a thousand gold-leaf butterflies
rise from dark trees.

She walks to the lake
and drinks the moon's reflection.
Undercurrents of summer

linger beneath the cold.
Deep in the bear's brain
lies a vision of winter,

the memory of snow.

Vow of Silence

To a mind that is still,
The whole universe surrenders.
          — Chuang Tzu

Distant brush fires seam
the mountainside—

smoke erases the moon.

Deep in the forest,
mute songbirds

settle in windless trees.

Under the earth,
tap roots

ration autumn rain.

Beneath the waves,
silent fish wait

for the lake to freeze.

Light

floods my camera lens,
as I search for a field
between over

and under.
When a leaf shadow
enters its green blade,

I press the shutter,
and a saving begins
of vein and stem

and broken gate.
A child's lost shoe,
an unopened letter.

Frail compositions
that will rise
from black.

Dowsing

Cut a forked branch.
Strip it clean of bark,

and hold fast.

Seeking water,
it leads you to places

you've never been.

The unseen
pulls like a ten pound trout

bending your branch earthward,

reeling in
the hidden spring.

Glass Doorway

If you stumble upon a glass door
hinged to a sturdy locust tree
in forests thick with sumac and pine,
know that my husband put it there.

An interactive sculpture
that moves not like a mobile
but a summer door,
opening and shutting

when the wind catches
its transparency.

On rainy days when the glass fogs,
you might draw watery glyphs
of fawn and cub with a wet finger
until the sun comes out.

In winter,
when snow falls on both sides,
the door might frost over,
framing an opaque universe

you're tempted
to knock on.

Cautious birds set sail
away from its silvered sky
and shuttered moon,
wondering if it's really better
on the other side.

The Poet Takes a Walk

An old woman I met by chance
said we'd not meet again
for a hundred years.

I look forward
to our reunion.

Grafton Street

Each time a coin chimes
inside the galvanized bucket,

the silver statue comes to life
and salutes the crowd.

Calliope music blares,
and the busker

lifts a plastic wand
to blow soap bubbles

that float aloft
like iridescent wishes

into the summer air.
A little girl chases after

the shimmering bubbles,
laughing and mesmerized

by their magic, always
just out of reach.

The Pheasant Grandfather

Appearing precisely after I thought unkindly of my grandfather,
the pheasant emerged as if on cue.
You, mother, who have filled my life with dreams,
would swear it was he.
The grandfather who once tamed another pheasant.
loved it, held it on his open hand,
the sun glistening off its green and red feathers.

The same grandfather, hunter, preacher's son
captured in a picture drunk out of his mind
with a hapless fawn sprawled in his lap.
The lion with the lamb, you always said.

But today it's just a pheasant,
alive and hiding in grass yellow with buttercup.
Not grandfather's soul called forth like some mute ghost,
and not the soul of his boyhood pet,
he later stuffed to forever perch on a fireplace mantle.
If I tell you this story,
you will dream the pheasant alive.

It will come within arm's reach
like the dead do in dreams.
You will sense that it's your father
and accept the truth of it

like a deer knows movement in a green meadow.
When the dream is over,
the pheasant will strut out of your mind
and out of this brisk June afternoon
in a country grandfather
never saw,
nor ever cared to see.

Went Missing

In the green of eternal autumn,
I walk into my shadow.

A collie friend lingers back this time,
not answering my call.

Moss covered rocks quarried years before
hold the morning rain.

A heifer bolts from a sleeping meadow
as if to stop me.

A sturdy colt nuzzles his pale mother,
watching from a safe distance.

Inisheer floats like vapor,
seaside lights are sequined far below.

Silence steals from horizon to dark horizon.
I lift smooth rocks from a limestone wall

to enter a strange field.
Stone by stone I put them back,

weighing the very heft of time,
closing the gate,

covering my tracks.

Beside the Corrib

Rushes line an ancient river.
A Viking dips his oar
into the dark.

Seagulls skim the waves.
White-winged salmon.

Sky for ceiling.
Nettles for doors.

Blackbirds seed the summer clouds.

Dissonance

Woody Guthrie is singing in Temple Bar.
Dylan Thomas passes me on the Ha' Penny Bridge.
On Grafton, a classical guitarist plays in front of a shoe store,
and I'm dancing at Lughnasa in Dublin under gun-metal skies.

The travellers with paper cups beg for pence,
and my father hurries by on O'Connell without a nod.
An artist paints a sidewalk masterpiece, and Madonna sings
This Used to be My Playground from the corner pub.

Molly Malone cries out on Moore Street
Tobacco! Bananas! Pears...six for a pound!
and I walk the streets of Dublin
past the dying children of King Lir and the ascending swans,

past a boy of seven and his chalk drawings
of pink hearts and green houses.
He looks up at me and smiles until a hard rain blurs
his colored sidewalk to gray sandpaper.

I give him a pound and a cock crows from St. Stephen's Green
and Mary sings of *a woman's heart*.
And mine, black as a tinker's, is baptized by 900 prayer candles
while Paula reads her witching poetry,

knowing this path by magic not by sight.
I rest on the edge of the Irish Sea
as the shadow of my hand crosses this page,
stitching and unstitching the wild swans that marked my way here

to the fuchsia that bleeds on Inish Mor where fishermen sail an ashen sea.
I listen on marbled currents for the matin bells to seed this feathered sky
with a vision where winter becomes summer,
where Lir's lovely daughter cradles her brothers in the fan of her wings

until the stain of death will wash away under night stars
in the silent Dublin rain.

Merrion Square

Once I slept in a poet's bed
while she was in France.
I climbed

the ladder to her tiny loft
to read about Killer Whales
and the nature of evil.

In the morning,
I bathed in her tub
and drank her red tea.

I stared at a picture
of a dark-eyed baby
and wondered

when does evil begin?
I locked the front door twice,
and descended a winding stair

that led me outside to a park.
I sat in the warm sun,
read random love poems,

and watched
a towheaded boy
play war.

FOR CLARE

Safe behind the blur of rain,
   you're writing blue words
on white paper.

A window holds the stormy Atlantic
   and craggy cliffs beyond.
Telephone poles

like glass chandeliers
   cross a Pegasus sky
pale with distance.

Fields of summer jigsaw as one,
   spiced with wildflowers
yet unnamed.

You rest your pen,
   light a candle in the gentian cup.
The wind waxes;

rain falls harder now.
   Words flicker like flame
as you brush your hair

one hundred times.
   You wind a ticking clock
until your thoughts flow blue.

The Cliffs of Moher

When the fog finally lifts,
teakwood arks jut into the ocean,
one after another, toward Hag's Head.

An old woman lies prostrate
on a sandstone ledge and stares
at the crashing waves 700 feet below.

Updrafts lift her long white hair
and for a second, it looks as if she's flying
over cushions of Sea Pink,

yellow Bird's-Foot Trefoil,
and scattered tuffets of Sea Campion
that dot the cliffside,

their white heads trembling
in the steady breeze.
Fulmars and Kittiwakes

hover like swarms of gnats,
and two sad-eyed Puffins with neon bills
keep watch from a grassy buttress.

As the sun sets in a burnt orange sky
and melts into a deepening sea,
the woman leaves no shadow,

the cliffs become silhouettes,
the ocean, a riot of sound.

Doolin

My father might have fit in here.
Evenings at McGann's,
loud laughter and song.
His family waiting

for the pubs to close.
It might have been all right:
his absence
over time.

Just another day,
another drunk
weaving down dark lanes
past Doonagore Castle.

The Atlantic singing in his ears.
Foxglove and clover
intoxicating the night.
The whiskey on his breath

leading him home.

On a Knoll on the West Coast of Ireland

A boy sits with his sister
who is learning to talk.
Their collie listens close by.

"Say sky," he commands,
pointing up
to a sea of sky.

"Say sea," he tells her,
pointing out
to a sky of sea.

She echoes each word
and waves her small finger
up and out

at the spreading blue tide.

Limerick

Behind the clock tower
stopped at 8:10pm,

a ten-story mural
of the Virgin Mary

stares back
with empty eyes.

But it's not Mary
or some saint

dressed in black,
shrouded in white.

It's the ghost face
of a young boy

with dark circles
under his eyes.

The weather vane
on the clock tower

points due North.
On the far shore

of the River Shannon,
a lone swan swims upstream.

We Walked in the Dark

all the way back,
me singing
half-remembered songs;

stray words
left fluttering
against streetlamps.

Under summer skies
the canal
guided us

through paved streets,
past row houses
asleep on unmoving tracks.

We went further.
Our feet grew accustomed
to earth.

Beyond sky and water
the same dusky gray,
the canal became a current.

We walked along the river
seeded with stars,
shadowed by bulrushes.

Silently we turned
in midnight flowers
and followed

the summer moon
pearled in the gray hand
of morning.

Author's Note

Journey with me from Appalachia to Ireland in *Looking for Ireland: An Irish-Appalachian Pilgrimage*. Millions of years ago the Appalachian Mountains spanned the Atlantic Ocean and became the Caledonia Mountains in Western Europe. When the Irish immigrated to Appalachia, the rolling green hills and mountains must have made them feel at home.

Since I was a child, I always dreamt of going to Ireland. My grandfather was born in Co. Galway and immigrated with his family to the United States. I have been lucky to visit Ireland four times and each stay seemed more wondrous than the last. I studied with Irish poets in Dublin at the Dublin Writing Workshop, the former U.S. poet laureate Billy Collins in Galway at the Galway Poetry Workshop, and spent a month as writer in residence in Co. Clare near the Cliffs of Moher. Recently, I traveled to Wales, Scotland, Northern Ireland, and returned once again to the Republic of Ireland.

The poems and photographs in this chapbook were created in West Virginia, western Maryland, and Ireland from 2000–2016. I enjoyed many solitary hours walking, reflecting, writing, and saving moments on this path, this journey, this magical pilgrimage.

Laura Treacy Bentley is a poet, novelist, and a point-and-shoot photographer. Born in Hagerstown, Maryland, she was raised in Huntington, West Virginia, and graduated from Marshall University. Laura divides her time between the mountains of West Virginia and a log cabin in western Maryland. To discover more about her, visit **lauratreacybentley.com**.

Acknowledgements

I am grateful to the editors of the following publications where these poems first appeared:

ABZ: "Glass Doorway."

California Quarterly: "We Walked in the Dark."

Connotations: An Online Artifact: "Swans, Tundra Swans" and "Signs."

Crannóg (Galway, Ireland) and *Wind*: "Amulets" and "Went Missing."

"Dissonance" was a finalist in the Scottish International Open Poetry Competition (Scotland).

Grey Sparrow Journal: "Vow of Silence." This poem was reprinted in *Eyes Glowing at the Edge of the Woods: Fiction and Poetry from West Virginia*.

"Late Autumn" was featured on Mountain Lines bus #295 in Morgantown, West Virginia.

Nightsun: "The Pheasant Grandfather."

Now & Then: "Dowsing." This poem was also featured on Poetry Daily.

Poetry Ireland Review (Dublin, Ireland): "Doolin" and "Beside the Corrib."

Some poems in this book are collected in *Lake Effect*: Huron, Ohio: Bottom Dog Press, 2006.

Glossary of Photos

COVER	The Cliffs of Moher, Co. Clare, Ireland
PAGE 3	"Waiting on Shore," Co. Sligo, Ireland
PAGE 5	McHenry, Maryland
PAGE 7	McHenry, Maryland
PAGE 9	Huntington, West Virginia
PAGE 10	Huntington, West Virginia
PAGE 12	Tobernalt Holy Well, Co. Sligo, Ireland
PAGE 13	Huntington, West Virginia
PAGE 14	Huntington, West Virginia
PAGE 16	Huntington, West Virginia
PAGE 19	Huntington, West Virginia
PAGE 20	Huntington, West Virginia
PAGE 21	The Aran Islands, Inish Mor, Ireland
PAGE 22	Dublin, Ireland — This photo inspired the novel *The Silver Tattoo*
PAGE 25	Huntington, West Virginia
PAGE 26	Co. Clare, Ireland
PAGE 29	McHenry, Maryland
PAGE 30	"The Children of Lir," Dublin, Ireland
PAGE 33	Belfast, Northern Ireland
PAGE 35	Co. Clare, Ireland
PAGE 36	The Cliffs of Moher, Co. Clare, Ireland
PAGE 39	Co. Clare, Ireland
PAGE 40	Ring of Kerry, Co. Kerry, Ireland
PAGE 41	Limerick, Ireland
PAGE 44	Huntington, West Virginia

www.ingramcontent.com/pod-product-compliance
Lightning Source LLC
Chambersburg PA
CBHW060809090426
42736CB00003B/209